TECHNICAL REPORT

A Survey of Qatari Secondary School Seniors

Methods and Results

Louay Constant • *Vazha Nadareishvili*

With
Hanine Salem

Prepared for the Supreme Education Council

RAND RAND-QATAR POLICY INSTITUTE

The research described in this report was prepared for the Supreme Education Council and conducted within the RAND-Qatar Policy Institute and RAND Education, programs of the RAND Corporation.

Library of Congress Cataloging-in-Publication Data

Constant, Louay.
    A survey of Qatari secondary school seniors : methods and results / Louay Constant, Vazha Nadareishvili.
      p. cm.
    Includes bibliographical references.
    ISBN 978-0-8330-4473-0 (pbk. : alk. paper)
    1. Education, Secondary—Qatar. 2. High school seniors—Qatar—Attitudes. 3. Student aspirations—Qatar. 4. College attendance—Qatar. 5. Vocational interests—Qatar. I. Nadareishvili, Vazha. II. Title.

LA1435.C66 2008
373.18095363—dc22

                                                                                    2008019236

The RAND Corporation is a nonprofit research organization providing objective analysis and effective solutions that address the challenges facing the public and private sectors around the world. RAND's publications do not necessarily reflect the opinions of its research clients and sponsors.

RAND® is a registered trademark.

Published 2008 by the RAND Corporation
1776 Main Street, P.O. Box 2138, Santa Monica, CA 90407-2138
1200 South Hayes Street, Arlington, VA 22202-5050
4570 Fifth Avenue, Suite 600, Pittsburgh, PA 15213-2665
RAND URL: http://www.rand.org/
To order RAND documents or to obtain additional information, contact
Distribution Services: Telephone: (310) 451-7002;
Fax: (310) 451-6915; Email: order@rand.org

Preface

The government of Qatar is embarking on a number of reforms to support the nation's economic and social development. Qatar's future depends on citizens whose education and training prepare them to be full participants in economic, social, and political life, and Qatar has made significant efforts to improve educational opportunities. Many efforts have focused on post-secondary education, but these individual initiatives have not been subject to a broader strategic review. Qatar's Supreme Education Council asked the RAND-Qatar Policy Institute (RQPI) to study the current situation and to help it identify priorities for developing post-secondary educational offerings that better respond to the country's economic and social demands.

This report presents the results of a survey of Qatari students enrolled in their final year of secondary school who expected to graduate in 2006. The survey focused on students' educational and career aspirations. It was carried out as part of a larger, one-year study of post-secondary education in Qatar. The report should be of interest to those concerned with education and economic development issues in the Middle East. It should also serve as a resource for researchers interested in the topic and findings of the survey.

The main report from this project is *Post-Secondary Education in Qatar: Employer Demand, Student Choice, and Options for Policy,* by Cathleen Stasz, Eric Eide, and Francisco Martorell, Santa Monica, Calif.: RAND Corporation, MG-644-QATAR, 2007. For detailed information on the survey administered to young Qataris who completed high school in 1998, see Francisco Martorell and Vazha Nadareishvili, *A Survey of Recent Qatar Secondary School Graduates: Methods and Results,* Santa Monica, Calif.: RAND Corporation, TR-578-QATAR, 2008.

This project was conducted under the auspices of RQPI and RAND's Education unit. RQPI is a partnership of the RAND Corporation and the Qatar Foundation for Education, Science, and Community Development. The aim of RQPI is to offer the RAND style of rigorous and objective analysis to clients in the greater Middle East. In serving clients in the Middle East, RQPI draws on the full professional resources of the RAND Corporation. RAND Education analyzes education policy and practice and supports implementation of improvements at all levels of the education system.

For further information on RQPI, contact the director, Dr. Richard Darilek. He can be reached by email at redar@rand.org; by telephone at +974-492-7400; or by mail at P.O. Box 23644, Doha, Qatar. For more information about RAND Education, contact the associate director, Dr. Charles Goldman. He can be reached by email at charlesg@rand.org; by telephone at +1-310-393-0411, extension 6748; or by mail at RAND, 1776 Main Street, Santa Monica, California 90401 USA.

Contents

Figure and Tables

Summary

Qatar has embarked on economic expansion and diversification initiatives that have created demand for skills and expertise in a wide range of fields. To date, however, this need has been filled largely by imported labor from abroad, which has resulted in a workforce that is predominately made up of foreign nationals. To reduce the nation's reliance on foreign labor in the growing oil and gas, technology, and services sectors, the leadership of Qatar has made substantial investments in post-secondary education and training in an effort to better prepare Qataris for the labor market.

In 2005, RAND was asked to study the post-secondary landscape and develop priorities for improving the opportunities available to Qataris to develop the skills that the nation needs. RAND developed a set of research questions designed to assess the extent to which current post-secondary opportunities intersect with employer demand for skills and the supply of skills among Qataris. An important component of this study was to examine the plans and aspirations of soon-to-be secondary school graduates of Qatar's education system. Up to that point, little in the way of systematically collected data existed to help understand the motivations behind decisions about pursuing post-secondary education and training, as well as long-term plans for employment. Therefore, RAND conducted a survey of students in their final year of secondary school.[1] These data, in addition to survey data collected on a random sample of young Qataris who graduated from secondary school in 1998, plus data on the secondary labor market and data from interviews with employers were analyzed to identify gaps in post-secondary opportunities and to recommend investment options (Stasz, Eide, and Martorell, 2007).

In this report, we examine data collected from the students in their final year of secondary school. Our main objective is to describe the survey and report its findings in more detail than provided in the study's main report.

Survey Design and Administration

The survey was primarily designed to ascertain the plans and aspirations of Qatari students in their final year of secondary school as they consider their options to enter the workforce or to continue on into post-secondary study. We employed a technique of random sampling of

---

[1] Students who participated in this survey anticipated graduating in spring 2006.

secondary schools stratified by gender and type (Independent, Ministry, private).[2] We then identified students in their final year who had reached age 18 at the time of the survey administration. The final sample consisted of 260 18-year-old third-year secondary school students (seniors) from Ministry schools, government-funded but autonomously operated Independent schools, and private Arabic schools. An important limitation of the sampling strategy was that it was designed to capture the diversity of schools in Qatar, and not necessarily the true numerical distribution of schools by type. Thus, students from Independent and private Arabic schools were overrepresented relative to students from Ministry schools. To take this issue into account, we calculated sampling weights using the 18-year-old student population distribution by gender across the different types of schools and then utilized those weights in the analysis.

Post-Secondary Plans of Qatari Secondary School Seniors

Significantly more females than males (60 percent versus 37 percent) plan to continue on into higher education after completing secondary school. Concomitantly, close to 50 percent of males plan to work after secondary school, compared with only 15 percent of females who plan to do the same. Males and females planned to make starkly different choices after graduating from secondary school, which suggests that they face very different post-secondary incentives—despite the fact that close to 60 percent of the males reported that they needed some post-secondary education or training to prepare them for their preferred job. The fact that Qataris can take advantage of further education and training opportunities after they have joined a government or government-owned organization may be part of the reason why the majority of males reported wanting to seek work first.

When asked about the type of organization they would prefer to work for, 75 percent of males said they preferred to work for a government ministry, compared with 33 percent for females. About 20 percent of males reported preferring a government-owned company, versus 27 percent of females who reported the same. Fewer than 2 percent of males reported preferring any kind of private organization, while close to 25 percent of females indicated they would work for a private organization, although mostly for a private charity or a religious organization, rather than for a private company.

We found similar differences between males and females when students were asked about their occupational preferences. Of those who specified an occupation (34 percent of the respondents), males overwhelmingly chose the military/police (65 percent), while females chose professional (33 percent), managerial (23 percent), and teaching (21 percent) occupations. The same pattern appeared when we examined occupational choice by post-secondary plan, particularly for males, where we found that the majority of students who indicated they do not plan to continue to post-secondary education plan to join the military or police. Students who do not plan to pursue post-secondary education also tended to prefer to work for a government ministry (65 percent) over other types of organizations such as government-owned organizations (16 percent) or those in the private sector (11 percent).

---

[2]   Independent schools are government-funded but privately operated. Ministry schools are both funded and operated by Qatar's Ministry of Education. Private schools are managed privately and typically do not receive operational funds from the government. However, some private schools implement Qatar's Ministry of Education curriculum, and students in their final year take the General Secondary School Certificate Examination (GSCE) to receive a high school degree.

Factors Affecting Post-Secondary Plans and Aspirations

Despite the differences between males and females in their plans, they report similar sources of influence in making their decisions. Both males and females cite parental advice and religious values as important drivers, and they see their parents mostly as facilitators in helping them get the job or career that they desire. Most females (56 percent) report societal views as being helpful in their job and career aspirations, suggesting that traditional views about the role of women in Qatar may be changing.

An important difference between males and females is in their perceptions of the extent to which their performance in school and mastery of skills would affect their ability to get the job they want. Females are significantly more likely than males to report that poor grades (21 percent versus 9 percent) and limited ability to converse in English (40 percent versus 15 percent) would hinder their ability to obtain the job or career they desire. Although a greater share of females than males (26 percent versus 12 percent) reported that low exit exam scores would hinder their ability to get the job they want, the difference was not significant at the 10-percent level ($p = 0.13$).

We found that, for the most part, males and females share the same feelings about the most important characteristics of a job or career. Both rate the prestige associated with a job or career, feelings of being respected on the job, and job security relatively high compared with other characteristics. There were some differences, however. Males tended to rate job benefits higher than females did, and females gave working hours greater importance than did males. One characteristic deemed important by both males and females was whether or not the job fostered a mixed-gender work environment. This suggests that both males and females look closely at the provisions organizations make in terms of mixed- or non-mixed-gender environments when seeking employment.

Student Awareness and Attitudes Toward Education and Work

Both males and females reported being aware of government scholarships and other types of resources that might support their post-secondary education and training pursuits. In general, they also consistently cited the same main sources of information on career and job opportunities—their parents, family, and the newspapers or television, less so their school or their teachers. Their attitudes toward education and career are also similar: They agree that doing well in school and getting a good education are important. Again, the main differences between males and females lie in their self-perceptions concerning job prospects. Whereas 59 percent of females are very certain they will get the job they want, more than 75 percent of males feel the same. Similarly, of the males who do not plan to pursue post-secondary education, 46 percent are very certain they will get the job they want, whereas of the females who do not plan to pursue post-secondary education only 10 percent are very certain they will get the job they want. These results suggest that males have considerably less incentive to pursue post-secondary education than do females.

Implications

For individuals interested in studying views and attitudes of Qatari students toward school and work, this report exemplifies how a survey can be conducted to collect this type of information. It describes the survey development process, population sampling procedure, and the logistics of administering the survey. It also provides a detailed description of sample representativeness and data properties. The study presented a unique opportunity to systematically collect primary data to analyze the attitudes and perceptions of young Qataris and the factors that influence their education and work decisions. This type of survey study is an important means of informing labor and education policy; if regularly carried out, it supplements existing labor force survey studies that are intended to gather general information about labor force participation and unemployment.

The report also reviews the most important findings from an analysis of these data. We examine the decisions Qatari students plan to make in their final year of secondary school about their post-secondary plans and the reasons behind these decisions. The results of this study are relevant to policymakers in Qatar who are evaluating strategies to meet human resource challenges through investments in post-secondary education and training initiatives. Analysis of responses given by Qatari students, especially the differences between males and females, suggests that those differences lie not in the value students place on education or training but in the incentives they face when deciding between multiple post-secondary options. If males are able to choose a high-paying and secure job that either provides them with education opportunities or eliminates the incentive to seek further education, they are likely to choose that option instead of continuing on to university. To further the goal of meeting the nation's long-term human resource needs, there should be a clear link between pursuing education and training opportunities and attaining competitive career and employment outcomes.

Acknowledgments

This report would not have been possible without the cooperation and support of a number of individuals and organizations. We are grateful for the full support and backing that we received from the Qatar Supreme Education Council (SEC), enabling us to carry out this study. We thank the Qatar Ministry of Education which provided the school data needed to carry out the sampling, as well as facilitated communication with Ministry and private Arabic schools to conduct the survey. The Education Institute similarly helped us gain access to administer the survey in the Independent schools. We thank the principals, teachers, and other officials at the schools for setting aside time and resources to allow us to administer the survey, as well as the students who took the time to complete them. We thank Dr. Eiman Al Ansari who carried out a number of crucial steps leading up to the full survey administration including collecting the information we needed to sample the students, contacting the schools, and the piloting of the survey. We are grateful for the work done by Hanine Salem (who organized all the field-work), Hessa Al Thani, Eiman Al Ansari, Reham El-Din Sayed, Mie Al Missned, Abdulrazaq Al Kuwari, and Joy Moini in administering the survey in the schools, and the efforts of Joy Moini and Lawrence Tingson in the post–survey administration processing. In Santa Monica, Joanna Nelsen, Jason Crooks, and Sharon Koga provided us with excellent administrative support that assisted us in completing the report.

We are also grateful to various RAND colleagues who provided intellectual guidance, feedback, and suggestions to improve this paper, namely Cathy Stasz, Paco Martorell, Charles Goldman, and Eric Eide. We also thank Laura Hamilton for coordinating quality assurance and Dominic Brewer and Larry Hanser for their detailed and insightful reviews.

Abbreviations

HEI	Qatar Higher Education Institute
KAHRAMAA	Qatar Water and Electricity Corporation
LFS	Qatar Labor Force Survey
MoE	Qatar Ministry of Education
QA	Qatar Airways
QP	Qatar Petroleum
Qtel	Qatar Telecommunications Corporation
RQPI	RAND-Qatar Policy Institute
SEC	Qatar Supreme Education Council

CHAPTER ONE

Introduction

Qatar has embarked on a number of large-scale initiatives to train more of the nation's citizens to take on the most important and sensitive jobs. This effort comes at a time when the country's main economic engine is run by a largely foreign labor force. This is especially the case in the professional and technical occupations: Current statistics suggest that the share of Qataris graduating from public schools who continue on to post-secondary study and/or training in these areas is far less than the anticipated needs of the country (Planning Council, 2005a).

Qataris also make up the largest share of the labor force in the government sector but a very small percentage of the labor force in the private sector. Labor force data collected from the Planning Council in 2004 reveal that around 50 percent of employees in the government sector (mainly ministries) were made up of Qatari nationals, in stark contrast to the private sector where less than 1 percent of the workforce is made up of Qataris. Qataris make up 27 percent of the labor force in government enterprises (government-owned) and only 20 percent of employees in the mixed sector, which is partially owned by the government (Planning Council, 2005a).[1] Qatar's leadership has been encouraging more citizens to find employment outside of the government ministries and in the growing government enterprise, mixed, and private sectors.

Training Qatari citizens in the appropriate sets of skills to meet demand in these growing sectors has been a concern of policymakers in Qatar for some time, and they have embarked on several major initiatives to address this issue (Qatar Foundation, 2008; Planning Council, 2005a). The nation has made significant post-secondary investments, including establishing branch campuses of major academic institutions of higher learning in Education City, opening a vocational college to provide specialized technical training in high-demand fields, and embarking on a major administrative and organizational reform of the national university.[2] A comprehensive reform of the K–12 education system is also taking place in Qatar (the Educa-

---

[1] The Planning Council also reports on the distribution of working Qataris across the different sectors. Of working Qataris, 77 percent are employed in the government sector, 13 percent in the government enterprise sector, 5 percent in the mixed sector, and 4 percent in the private sector (Planning Council, 2005a, Table 2.10, p. 41). Government enterprises include such organizations as Qatar Petroleum (QP), Qatar Telecommunications Corporation (Qtel), and Qatar Water and Electricity Corporation (KAHRAMAA). Qatar Airways (QA) is considered to be in the mixed sector since it is split between government and private ownership.

[2] Branch campuses in Education City include the Virginia Commonwealth University School of Design–Qatar (VCU-Q), the Weill Cornell Medical College, Carnegie-Mellon University–Qatar (CMU-Q), Texas A&M University–Qatar (TAMU-Q), and Georgetown University. These institutions offer undergraduate programs, with the exception of Weill Cornell Medical College, which offers a combined six-year undergraduate pre-med and graduate medical program. Northwestern University (Evanston, Illinois) is the most recent addition, offering undergraduate programs in media and communications beginning fall of 2008. The College of the North Atlantic (CNA), which focuses on post-secondary voca-

tion for a New Era reform), and plans for additional education and labor reforms are being laid out. These efforts are intended to ensure that Qataris are trained in areas of high demand to meet the growing future human resource needs of the country.

With these initiatives well under way, the government of Qatar commissioned a study to examine whether these efforts are meeting their objectives of providing viable post-secondary options for secondary school students as they consider their plans after graduation. By *viable* we mean options that are consistent with the skills needs of the nation while at the same time attractive to secondary school graduates. Part of this study was an attempt to understand the motivations of young people as they consider their post-secondary options and the drivers behind decisions to continue to obtain additional schooling and/or training. During the 2005–2006 academic year, RAND conducted a comprehensive study of post-secondary options in Qatar to address a set of overarching questions:

1. In which occupations can Qataris make the greatest contribution to the society and economy, and what education and training are needed to realize those contributions?
2. What measures might encourage more Qataris, especially young men, to pursue post-secondary education?
3. To what extent do existing institutions meet education and training needs? Where are new investments required?
4. What are the benefits and costs of establishing local post-secondary institutions, at both the undergraduate and graduate levels, versus sending students abroad?

The study included interviews with higher education officials and major employers in government, government enterprises, and the private sector to identify the types of skills that are in demand in Qatar. Data were also collected on post-secondary education and enrollment trends. The study also surveyed Qataris who graduated from secondary school in 1998 to learn about their post–high school education and employment experiences.[3] Finally, it surveyed secondary school seniors to learn about their planned career choices and aspirations, as well as their attitudes about further education and work. The results of this comprehensive study have been published in *Post-Secondary Education in Qatar: Employer Demand, Student Choice, and Options for Policy* (Stasz, Eide, and Martorell, 2007).

In this report, we focus on the results of the survey of secondary school seniors, with two main objectives in mind. Our first objective is to provide information on attitudes and aspirations of soon-to-be graduates of Qatar's secondary schools. This information could be useful to individuals seeking to understand the education and career choices made by soon-to-be secondary school graduates and the factors affecting those choices. Our second objective is to provide a more complete documentation of the survey and its findings, beyond that reported in Stasz, Eide, and Martorell, 2007. The data presented here may be of use to researchers in other countries besides Qatar.

The results of the survey of secondary school seniors contribute to existing knowledge about national labor force trends, such as those collected in the Qatar Labor Force Survey

---

tional training, was established in 2002, and the reform of the country's national university, Qatar University (QU), began in 2003 (Qatar University, 2007).

[3] For a detailed analysis of the 1998 survey of young Qataris, see the complementary report, Martorell and Nadareishvili (2008).

(LFS). The most recent administration of LFS by the General Secretariat for Development Planning in Qatar (previously, the Planning Council) occurred at around the same time as the administration of RAND's survey of secondary school seniors (in March 2006).[4] This analysis, on the other hand, examines in more depth the conditions under which Qatari seniors make important decisions about education, career, and work. We analyze the responses of Qatari high school seniors on a number of important post-secondary dimensions:

- preferences for careers and employers
- factors affecting post-secondary education and work decisions
- preferences for job features and work environment characteristics
- general attitudes toward education and work
- knowledge of post-secondary education scholarships and training and job opportunities.

These dimensions are important when considering different options for national post-secondary planning. General surveys of labor force participation and unemployment, such as the LFS, are essential for macro-level labor force planning and policymaking. On the other hand, the results from RAND's survey of 2006 secondary school seniors shortly before their graduation helps planners understand the reasons behind choices regarding education and work and illuminates options for addressing the underlying factors affecting those decisions.

The report is divided into six chapters. In Chapter Two, we describe the methodology we used to collect and process the data and the basic characteristics of those data. We also discuss the development of the survey, the sampling frame, the survey administration, the post-administration data entry process, and the representativeness of the sample. Chapter Three provides information on the respondents' family background and their post-secondary plans. Chapter Four discusses the responses of students on the factors they report affecting their post-secondary career plans, including personal and social circumstances, along with the barriers to, and facilitators of, pursuing their career of choice. Chapter Five analyzes student awareness and attitudes toward education and work, including access to post-secondary scholarships and sources of information on career opportunities. Chapter Six provides concluding thoughts. The survey instrument and an explanation of the procedure for weighting the sample are included for reference in Appendixes A and B, respectively.

---

[4] For a detailed review of the General Secretariat's 2006 Labor Force Survey, see General Secretariat for Development Planning, State of Qatar (2007).

CHAPTER TWO

Methodology

In this chapter, we explain the methodology employed to collect the data, beginning with the survey design and administration and followed by the sampling procedure. After that, a discussion ensues concerning the characteristics of the sample and its representativeness. We also describe the methods we used to analyze the data.

Survey Design and Administration

The student survey was designed to gather information about secondary school students' educational and career aspirations and the factors that may affect those aspirations. The survey began with background questions, including date of birth, gender, nationality (Qatari or non-Qatari), course of study, current grade, year in current grade (first time or repeating grade), and father's and mother's level of education. The second part of the survey first asked students about their plans for the future, such as what they planned to do directly after graduating from secondary school and what factors influenced those plans (e.g., parental advice, religious beliefs, societal expectations).

Students were then asked several questions about work and career, including what type of job they would like to have, the preparation they would need to reach their career goals, and the type of organization in which they would like to work (e.g., government, government enterprise, private company, or charity). Responses to these questions provide a sense of student attitudes toward education and work.

Students were also asked questions about the importance of different job characteristics in their potential choice of a job, such as salary, work environment, benefits, and the level of difficulty associated with the job. Students were also asked about factors that might help or hinder them in achieving their career goals and for their opinions on a number of statements about school and work. These items were designed to gather some empirical data that could support or refute opinions of employers and others about what motivates young Qataris.

The draft survey was written in English and then translated into Arabic. A member of the research team pilot-tested the survey at two schools, after which some revisions were made to the Arabic translation. The revisions were in turn back-translated to English to ensure that the Arabic and English versions matched as closely as possible. The final survey included 18 items and took about one-half hour to complete. Students completed the survey anonymously.

The first item of the survey asked the respondents to specify their date of birth, which allowed us to double-check that students were at least 18 years old on their last birthday and therefore would not need parental permission to complete the survey.[1]

The survey was closed-ended, except that students were asked to write in the kind of job they would most like to have.[2] These written responses were translated into English, and completed surveys were entered into electronic format for data analysis. The survey is provided in Appendix A.

Sampling Procedure

We employed a stratified sampling strategy to select schools, with stratification based on school gender (male and female schools) and school type.[3] We randomly selected 10 secondary schools: four Ministry of Education (MoE) schools, two Generation I Independent schools, three Generation II Independent schools, and one private school.[4] This selection reflects the diversity of K–12 schools in Qatar, typically differentiated by governance (the oversight institution) and funding (government versus private). A brief description of each of these types of schools is provided below.

- Ministry of Education schools operate under the direct supervision of the Qatar Ministry of Education.
- Independent schools, which have been in operation since September 2004, are publicly funded and operate under contract to the SEC. These schools are part of a recent K–12 education reform initiative to offer more government schooling options. Generation I schools opened in 2004, and Generation II schools opened in 2005.
- Private schools are fee-charging education organizations operated as private enterprises. These schools operated under license from the Ministry of Education at the time of the survey administration.

---

[1] Because we surveyed students older than 18, we did not require parental permission. Given the short time span and other demands of the larger study, we were concerned that this process could cause delays in data collection. We expect that for the purposes of this survey, age does not, in and of itself, affect how students would respond about their attitudes and motivations toward post-secondary education and work. For context, Table 2.2 provides information on the total number of male and female Qatari secondary students (older than 15) across the four types of secondary schools.

[2] The write-in responses for preferred job were recoded to fit into the International Standard Classification of Occupations–88 (ISCO-88).

[3] Most schools in Qatar are separated by gender. Type of school refers to Ministry of Education, Independent, and private Arabic schools.

[4] Generation I Independent schools were the first schools established as part of the Supreme Education Council's (SEC's) Education for a New Era reform. Generation II schools were the second cohort of schools established under the auspices of the SEC. Generation I numbered 12 schools, and Generation II numbered 21 schools. When the survey was administered in spring of 2006, only Generations I and II Independent schools had been established. Two of the schools in Generation I were scientific schools, which were more highly selective government schools with a math and science focus. Our sample included students from both the boys' and girls' scientific schools. Beginning in fall 2008, there will be five Generations (79 primary, preparatory, and secondary schools, as well as three stand-alone kindergartens) to make a total of 82 Independent schools (Supreme Education Council, 2008b).

While these schools were representative of the types of schools in Qatar, the numbers of schools in the sample did not reflect the true proportion of schools by type in Qatar. We over-sampled both Independent schools and private Arabic schools. Table 2.1 provides information on the total number of schools by type in Qatar, and the number of schools in our sample. To account for the fact that we oversampled certain schools, we weighted responses in our analysis based on the number of students enrolled in each of these different types of schools in the population. We describe this in more detail in the next section. Due to scheduling conflicts, we were unable to obtain permission to administer the survey in a private Arabic girls' school.

Once schools were selected, we utilized a database provided by the Ministry of Education of students in their third (final) year of secondary school in each of the MoE, Independent, and private Arabic sampled schools to identify those students who were older than 18 at the time of survey administration. A list of student names was generated and provided to the principals of the sampled schools, who set aside a class period and classroom to administer the survey. Age-eligible students who were in attendance the day of the administration participated on a voluntary basis. Virtually every student agreed to participate.

Table 2.1
Distribution of Secondary Schools, by Type, Spring 2006

Type of School	Total Number		Sample Number	
	Male	Female	Male	Female
Private Arabic	5	6	1	—
Ministry of Education	17	22	2	2
Independent, Generation I	2	1	1	1
Independent, Generation II	2	2	1	2
Total	26	31	5	5

Characteristics and Representativeness of the Sample

The sample consisted of 260 respondents—107 males and 153 females. The mean age in years was 19.0 for males and 19.1 for females.[5] The survey administration was designed to include only Qatari students as identified through the Ministry of Education database, although one student responded as not being Qatari.

Table 2.2 provides information on the representativeness of the sample. The population from which the sample was drawn consists of the number and percentage of 18-year-old students (during the time of the survey administration) in their final year of secondary school in each of the different types of schools. The "Sample" column represents the distribution within our sample. Qatari males in private Arabic schools were overrepresented relative to the population (6 percent in the sample compared to 3 percent in the population). The same holds true for Generation I and Generation II Independent schools for both Qatari males and females.

---

[5] Adjusting age for weights did not significantly change the average age at 19.0 for males and 19.2 for females.

Table 2.2
Distribution of Qatari Secondary School Seniors, by School Type

School Type	Male (18+ years)				Female (18+ years)				Male (15+ years)		Female (15+ years)	
	Population		Sample		Population		Sample		Population		Population	
	Number	%	Number	%	Number	%	Number	%	Number	%	Number	%
Private Arabic	21	3	6	6	—	—	—	—	70	5	—	—
Ministry of Education	580	84	74	69	674	92	110	72	1,108	76	1,804	86
Independent Generation I	4	1	4	4	7	1	7	5	73	5	138	7
Independent Generation II	84	12	23	21	52	7	36	23	201	14	154	7
Total	689	100	107	100	733	100	153	100	1,452	100	2,096	100

NOTE: A private Arabic girls' school was not included in the sample. All numbers include only Qataris.

To provide additional context, the table also includes information about the population of all Qatari secondary students (15+ years of age) enrolled in the four types of schools.

To take into account that students in certain types of schools were overrepresented in comparison to the population, we weighted responses in reference to the population distribution of 18-year-old male and female students across the types of schools in Qatar. Students from a school that was oversampled were weighted downward because they represented a larger share of the sample than they do in the population, and vice versa for a student whose school was undersampled relative to the population distribution. The resulting weights were used in the data analysis discussed in the subsequent sections (see Appendix B for weight formula and resulting weights used in the calculations).

Approach to Analysis

Our analysis of the data consisted of creating tabulations of responses to the survey questions, illustrating the results in almost all cases by gender. This was done to highlight the differences between males and females, an issue relevant to policymakers in Qatar. Since we employed a stratified sampling strategy, we account for respondent clustering around schools in the analysis and computed clustered standard errors. Statistical tests (adjusted Wald-tests) were utilized where appropriate to determine whether differences were statistically significant. We cite results of significance tests by reporting p-values associated with analysis of differences between groups. In general, a significance level of 0.05 was used throughout.

CHAPTER THREE

Parent Education and Post-Secondary Plans

In this chapter, we report on parent education and students' post-secondary plans and aspirations. We discuss the main differences between males' and females' education and career plans. We conclude the chapter by showing how students who plan to pursue post-secondary education compare with those who do not, in terms of their career choice and the type of organization they see themselves working in.

Parents' Educational Attainment

Students were asked to report on their parents' educational level in the survey, since studies indicate that parents' education is correlated with student outcomes and is a proxy for student background and level of family resources (Mortimer, Dennehy, and Lee, 1992; The Minnesota High School Follow-Up Survey, 2000, 2001; Gouvias and Vitsilakis-Soroniatis, 2005; Need and de Jong, 2001; DeRidder, 1990). Parents who are highly educated could provide greater access to information about post-secondary options and could have higher expectations for their children's education. In this report, we provide information on parent education as a measure of home context, but we do not attempt to link it directly to student choices or outcomes. Thus, we cannot say for sure that parent education is linked to student outcomes in the same way as other studies have found in different contexts. However, in future empirical studies examining correlates of student outcomes, parent education would be an important variable to include.

Table 3.1 shows the level of student-reported parent education for males and females. Only 15 percent of males' and females' fathers and 7 percent of their mothers had pursued

Table 3.1
Parents' Education, by Gender (%)

Educational Level	Father's Education			Mother's Education		
	Male	Female	Total	Male	Female	Total
No schooling	29.1	24.3	26.6	45.8	44.2	44.9
Primary	29.5	27.0	28.2	27.2	25.9	26.5
Preparatory	18.0	25.0	21.6	9.5	15.2	12.4
Secondary	6.5	10.0	8.3	7.6	9.7	8.7
Post-secondary	16.8	13.7	15.2	9.9	5.1	7.4
Sample size	100	144	244	101	150	251

post-secondary education, and most of the students' fathers (55 percent) and mothers (71 percent) were reported as having only primary-level or no schooling. For comparison purposes, these numbers indicate that student-reported parent education level in Qatar is considerably below the international averages reported by eighth graders from the nations participating in the 2003 Third International Mathematics and Science Study (TIMSS). In that study, 45 percent of the students reported their parents as having received some type of post-secondary education and only 12 percent of students reported their parents as having completed only primary or no schooling (Mullis et al., 2004, p. 126).

Students' Post-Secondary Education Aspirations

We asked students to tell us about their plans after graduation from secondary school. Their responses provide a projection of potential patterns of further study or employment preferences of soon-to-be secondary school graduates (Table 3.2). The results show that 60 percent of females versus 37 percent of males (p = 0.013) plan to attend university, whereas 49 percent of males and 15 percent of females (p < 0.01) indicated that they would go to work right after secondary school.

The significant disparity in the share of females versus males planning to pursue post-secondary study has much to do with the fact that women face different opportunities and incentives in their career planning. Traditionally, the teaching profession has been one of the few career options available to women, and it requires a post-secondary degree. On the other hand, males have many more options, including jobs that do not require a post-secondary degree (e.g., military or police). Thus they have fewer incentives to seek post-secondary education and training (see Stasz, Eide, and Martorell, 2007, for further discussion). Although a greater share of females (14 percent) compared with males (7 percent) reported being unsure of what they will do after graduation, the difference was not statistically significant (p = 0.19).

Students' Career Aspirations

We also asked students what types of organizations they would most like to work in when they are ready to join the workforce (Table 3.3). This question allowed us to compare the employment preferences of soon-to-be secondary school graduates with the Qatari leadership's goal to increase employment of Qatari nationals in the private and government enterprise

Table 3.2
Post-Secondary Plans of Secondary School Students (%)

Plan	Male	Female	Total
Go to university	37.3	60.0	49.1
Go to technical college	3.5	7.1	5.4
Go to work right after high school	48.8	15.1	31.3
Not sure what I will do	6.9	14.0	10.6
Other	3.4	3.8	3.6
Sample size	103	152	255

Table 3.3
Desired Employer Type, by Gender (%)

Employer	Male	Female	Total
Government ministry	74.6	32.8	53.6
Government-owned company	20.5	26.6	23.6
Private charity/religious organization	1.2	18.3	9.8
Private company	0.6	6.2	3.4
Unsure	3.1	16.1	9.6
Sample size	96	133	229

sectors. The results suggest that a large gap exists between national goals and student plans, especially in the case of males. Seventy-five percent of males indicated that they would like to work in the government sector, compared with 33 percent of females (p < 0.01). A significant share of females would work in government enterprises (27 percent), and almost as many of them (24 percent) would work in the private sector, although primarily for private charitable and religious organizations (18 percent out of 24 percent) rather than for private companies. On the other hand, very few males chose the private sector, and only 21 percent chose the government enterprise sector. In general, the government sector is preferred because it offers amenities that are not available in the private sector, such as job security, shorter working hours, and better benefits (Planning Council, 2005a). These results suggest that employers in the private noncharitable and nonreligious sectors will continue to face challenges in recruiting both Qatari females and males.

We asked students about their occupational and career aspirations, to get a general sense of how well they aligned with growth in labor demand in the professional, technical, and services fields where demand is greatest (Stasz, Eide, and Martorell, 2007). Only 34 percent of male and female respondents reported specific occupational preferences; the remaining 66 percent marked "unsure," "I do not plan to obtain a job," or "I do not have an answer." Although we would like to say something about the occupational choices of those who did indicate one in the survey, we must interpret the responses to this question with caution, given that the majority did not specify an occupation at all. We report the results in Table 3.4. Note that in Table 3.4, we include the share of respondents who did not specify an occupation ("Unsure" or "Do not plan to get a job"). If we were to exclude the "Unsure" and "Do not plan to get a job" categories, we would find that almost two-thirds of the males (65 percent) who reported an occupational preference indicated they would join the military or the police; only around 13 percent had aspirations to become a professional, such as a doctor, lawyer, or scientist. For females who did specify an occupation, occupational and career aspirations were more evenly distributed across different types of professions compared with males, who disproportionately favored the military or police.

The relatively low share of males planning on continuing with post-secondary study may be explained to some extent by the share of males planning to join the military or police. Currently, a post-secondary degree is not required to join the military or police, and this apparently attractive option may be precluding Qatari males from seeking post-secondary education. Government enterprises, such as Qatar Petroleum (QP), also provide their own training

Table 3.4
Desired Occupation, by Gender (%)

Occupation	Male	Female	Total
Associate professional	2.6	1.9	2.2
Clerk	0.0	1.0	0.5
Engineer	1.6	3.4	2.5
Legislator/senior officer/manager	3.3	7.4	5.4
Military or police	23.1	0.2	11.2
Professional	4.5	10.8	7.8
Service worker	0.0	1.0	0.5
Teacher	0.6	7.0	3.9
Do not plan to get a job	3.3	3.1	3.2
Unsure[a]	61.1	64.2	62.7
Sample size	103	152	255

[a] The "Unsure" category includes those who responded "Unsure" or "I do not have an answer."

programs, so some of the responses may reflect an understanding that education and training will be received through employment. Females who specified an occupation in their response to the question indicated nonteaching professional (33 percent), legislator/senior officer/manager (23 percent), and teaching professional (21 percent) as their main career preferences, all of which typically require a post-secondary degree.[1] In Chapter Four, we examine the factors that males and females find important in their selection of a career, and the conditions they factor in when selecting a job or career.

Students' Perceptions Toward Post-Secondary Education

One of the main motivations for our larger study was to examine the types of education and training that are needed to prepare students to join the workforce. Through interviews with employers, the study found that the most sought-after skills for job candidates were English-language ability, knowledge of information and communications technology, and business skills, all of which are obtained through post-secondary training (Stasz, Eide, and Martorell, 2007). To see whether students thought they needed additional training, they were asked what kind of preparation they would need to be ready for a job. Table 3.5 shows that students felt that getting a university degree or other type of training was indeed important for the job they preferred (32.3 percent for males and 38.0 percent for females); more females than males (24 percent versus 18 percent) felt that work experience was all that was needed to feel adequately prepared for the job.

While only 41 percent of males planned to pursue some kind of post-secondary education or qualification (university or technical college—the first two rows in Table 3.2), almost 60 percent felt that a university degree (obtained in Qatar or abroad) or other qualification would be needed to adequately prepare them for their preferred job. On the other hand, most females

---

[1]   These figures refer only to the 33 percent of females who did not select "Unsure" or "Do not plan to get a job" and specified an occupation in their response to the question.

Table 3.5
Preparation Needed for the Most Preferred Job (%)

Type of Preparation	Male	Female	Total
University degree in Qatar	32.3	38.0	35.2
University degree abroad	21.1	16.5	18.8
Other qualification	6.1	2.2	4.1
Work experience	18.1	24.2	21.2
No further preparation needed	3.0	2.7	2.9
Not sure what preparation needed	8.5	9.0	8.8
Other	2.9	0.9	1.9
Do not plan to work	3.7	0.9	2.2
Don't know	4.2	5.6	4.9
Sample size	99	141	240

(67 percent, see Table 3.2) planned to continue into post-secondary education (either university or technical college), even though only around 57 percent of them felt that gaining a university degree or other qualification was necessary to obtain their preferred jobs. This suggests that even if males recognize the need for additional training, they are opting for careers in fields that do not require a post-secondary degree. It could also be that they believe they will get the training and skills they need through direct employment first, although this explanation is not directly supported in the data collected from secondary school students.

Occupational Choice and Post-Secondary Education

We also wanted to assess differences in career choices based on whether students intended to pursue post-secondary education or not. The differences between these two groups is as expected: A much greater share of students (primarily males) who are not planning to pursue post-secondary education opt for the military or police, whereas a greater percentage of those who do plan on pursuing post-secondary education opt for careers as engineers, legislators/senior officers/managers, professionals, and teachers. We also note that a greater percentage of students who did not intend to pursue post-secondary education or training were unsure of the occupation they wanted to pursue, compared with those who did intend to (Table 3.6).

We also examined how students who plan to pursue post-secondary studies compared with those who do not in terms of where they plan to work (Table 3.7). The greatest difference between these two groups is in their preference for government (Ministry) versus government enterprises. Although 50 percent of students who planned to further their schooling preferred to work in a government ministry, this preference was shared by up to 65 percent of those who do not plan to pursue post-secondary schooling ($p = 0.05$). Twenty-eight percent of those who planned to continue their schooling prefer to work in a government-owned company compared with just 16 percent of those who do not plan to continue their schooling ($p < 0.05$). Of those who do not plan to pursue post-secondary education, none planned to work for a private company.

Table 3.6
Occupation, by Post-Secondary Plan (%)

Occupation	Post-Secondary Education Wanted	Post-Secondary Education Not Wanted	Unsure	Total
Associate professional	1.9	1.8	4.4	2.2
Clerk	0.9	0.0	0.0	0.5
Engineer	4.8	0.0	0.0	2.5
Legislator; senior officer; manager	7.2	2.0	6.3	5.4
Military or police	6.0	24.0	2.1	11.2
Professional	11.4	2.0	7.1	7.8
Service worker	0.0	0.0	3.5	0.5
Teacher	6.2	0.4	3.5	3.9
Do not plan to get a job	5.1	1.6	0.0	3.2
Unsure[a]	56.5	68.3	73.1	62.7
Sample size	147	71	37	255

[a] The "Unsure" category includes those who responded "Unsure" or "Do not have an answer."

Table 3.7
Desired Work Sector, by Post-Secondary Plan (%)

Sector	Post-Secondary Education Wanted	Post-Secondary Education Not Wanted	Unsure	Total
Ministry	50.0	65.1	42.4	53.6
Government-owned company	28.4	16.2	21.4	23.6
Private charity or religious organization	7.1	11.2	16.9	9.8
Private company	6.2	0.0	0.0	3.4
Unsure	8.3	7.5	19.3	9.6
Sample size	131	63	35	229

Our findings in this chapter show that the differences between males and females in terms of post-secondary plans have to do with the incentives they face when deciding about pursuing post-secondary education. Whether or not post-secondary education is needed to obtain a good job appears to be the driving force behind males' and females' plans after graduation. The military or police, an attractive occupational choice for Qatari males, may be one reason why males do not plan to pursue post-secondary education.

We next explore the factors that males and females consider when choosing a career, to better understand why they may prefer some job options over others.

CHAPTER FOUR

Factors Affecting Post-Secondary Plans, Perceived Barriers and Facilitators, and Preferences in Job Characteristics

In the previous chapter, we reported on students' post-secondary education aspirations and career plans. In this chapter, we present survey findings on the relative importance that students place on various personal and social factors in deciding on their post-secondary plans, as well as their perceptions of barriers and facilitators to achieving desired jobs or careers. We also provide the results of examining the importance respondents place on different characteristics of a job and work environment to better understand what matters to them when searching for employment.

Factors Affecting Post-Secondary Plans

In order to understand the underlying factors influencing career-related decisions, we asked students about preferences related to career and work-related choices. We asked students to rate factors along a four-point scale, ranging from "not important" to "extremely important". More than 90 percent of both males and females rated their parents' advice and their religious beliefs as very important or extremely important in setting their career and work goals. The only factor that fewer than half the respondents found very or extremely important was advice from friends. We summarize the findings in Table 4.1, which provides the average score given to each factor by males and females and how those scores were ranked.

Males and females are in agreement on the importance of parental advice and religious values in deciding on their career plans, ranking these factors as most influential. Parental advice is, however, more important for males compared with females—mean score for males is 3.79, and for females it is 3.58 ($p < 0.01$). Table 4.1 shows that the responses of males and females are consistent on the other factors as well: They generally rate each factor as of similar importance relative to the others. The only slight differences were in getting a scholarship and receiving advice from other family members, where statistically significant differences between mean scores for male and female respondents were found only at the 10-percent level (scholarship, 3.20 and 2.98, respectively, $p = 0.089$; and family, 2.81 and 2.67, $p = 0.063$).

Table 4.1
Factors That Affect Post-Secondary Plans, by Gender

Factor	Male			Female			Total		
	Mean	Std. Err.	Rank	Mean	Std. Err.	Rank	Mean	Std. Err.	Rank
Personal interests	3.34	0.03	4	3.47	0.08	3	3.41	0.05	4
Advice from father or mother	3.79	0.03	1	3.58	0.03	2	3.68	0.05	2
Other family members	2.81	0.06	8	2.67	0.01	8	2.74	0.04	8
Advice from friends	2.49	0.06	9	2.47	0.12	9	2.48	0.07	9
Religious beliefs	3.74	0.02	2	3.78	0.05	1	3.76	0.03	1
Societal expectations	3.18	0.06	6	3.11	0.09	5	3.14	0.05	5
Enjoyment of learning and school	2.88	0.18	7	2.98	0.04	7	2.93	0.09	7
Kinds of jobs that are open to you	3.48	0.05	3	3.45	0.04	4	3.47	0.03	3
Whether you get a scholarship	3.20	0.09	5	2.98	0.07	6	3.09	0.07	6
Sample size	103			152			255		

NOTE: Each factor was scored by respondents as "not important" (1), "somewhat important" (2), very important" (3), "extremely important" (4), or "don't know" (0). Scores are calculated as means after dropping "don't know" responses. Sample size varies slightly across questions. Standard errors are reported.

Perceived Barriers and Facilitators to Job and Career Preferences

Different factors may help or hinder a person in attaining a job or career of his or her choice. We presented respondents with a number of such factors and asked them to say which ones they perceived as supportive, which they considered would prevent them from obtaining the job or career of their choice, and which would neither support nor prevent them (see Table 4.2).

Most males and females felt that their parents would help them in attaining the job or career of their choice, although more females than males (19.6 percent versus 3.5 percent, $p < 0.01$) felt that they neither helped nor prevented. A smaller share of females than males responded that other members of their family would help them in getting the job or career of their choice (54.8 percent versus 66.7 percent, $p < 0.05$). A greater share of females than males indicated that other members of their family would prevent them from getting the job or career of their choice (9.8 percent versus 1.2 percent, $p < 0.01$), while males were more likely than females to see their friends as posing a barrier (10.5 percent versus 1.7 percent, $p < 0.05$). This suggests that females may face more pressure from family whereas males face more pressure from friends when making job or career plans.

Females and males also differed in their perception of how their performance in school and their skills affect their ability to get a job or career. A smaller share of males compared with females reported that their grades and their English language skills would hinder their ability to get a job or career: 8.9 percent versus 21.1 percent ($p < 0.05$) for grades, and 15.3 percent versus 39.7 percent ($p < 0.01$) for English skills, respectively. On the other hand, while a smaller share of males than females reported that their exit exam scores would hinder their

Table 4.2
Barriers and Facilitators to Getting the Job or Career Desired (%)

Factors	Male			Female			Total		
	Prevent	Neither Help nor Prevent	Help	Prevent	Neither Help nor Prevent	Help	Prevent	Neither Help nor Prevent	Help
My personal interests	4.1	36.7	57.7	4.6	31.6	59.3	4.3	34.0	58.5
My parents	0.0	3.5	94.1	3.5	19.6	74.8	1.8	11.9	84.1
Other members of my family	1.2	28.6	66.7	9.8	32.5	54.8	5.6	30.6	60.5
My friends	10.5	45.3	40.7	1.7	39.8	53.6	5.9	42.5	47.4
My school or teachers	5.8	40.2	48.8	7.8	44.5	39.8	6.8	42.4	44.1
My grades in school	8.9	21.4	67.4	21.1	29.7	46.2	15.3	25.8	56.2
My exam scores	12.3	18.7	67.8	25.7	17.9	53.6	19.3	18.3	60.4
My willingness to work hard	1.7	11.8	85.4	5.4	11.9	80.6	3.6	11.8	82.9
Family obligations	4.8	39.6	49.8	9.0	32.7	54.3	7.0	36.0	52.2
Societal views about women in the workforce	20.3	38.9	31.0	10.2	28.3	56.1	15.1	33.4	44.0
Personal contacts	4.1	32.5	60.6	4.8	19.5	69.2	4.4	25.8	65.0
What I studied in school	8.3	25.5	63.9	7.1	21.0	68.1	7.7	23.2	66.1
My ability to speak English	15.3	19.8	63.8	39.7	13.2	45.4	28.0	16.4	54.2
My ability to get along with other people	1.7	24.4	73.9	7.0	20.0	71.3	4.4	22.1	72.5
Sample size		103			152			255	

NOTE: Sample size varies slightly across questions.

ability to get their preferred job or career (12.3 percent versus 25.7 percent), the difference was not statistically significant at the 10-percent level (p = 0.13).[1] Nonetheless, the results suggest that males see fewer barriers to getting a job than do females. While career opportunities for Qatari women are expanding, they may still perceive greater competition than do Qatari men for job positions. Despite increases in Qatari female labor force participation, Qatari women remain concentrated in education and government administration jobs, although this could change as education opportunities continue to expand and women pursue higher education in science, business, and technology fields (Planning Council, 2005a).

Most females responded that societal views about women in the workforce had helped their job and career aspirations (56 percent), while 10 percent felt that it was a hindrance, and 28 percent felt it had no effect. This and the previous finding are consistent with a study that notes that changing societal views in Qatar are breaking down barriers that used to prevent women from seeking opportunities to participate in the workforce and pursue careers historically reserved for men (Bahry and Marr, 2005). In Chapter Five of this report, we will exam-

---

[1]   All students in the government and private Arabic schools must pass an exit exam in their final year of secondary school before they can graduate. The student's score on the exit exam is used to determine admission into Qatar University and eligibility for a government scholarship to study abroad. It can also be used by both government and private-sector employers to determine job placement.

ine views on female participation in the workforce to see whether these attitudes are reflected among young generations of Qataris.

Preferences in Work Conditions and Job Characteristics

We also wanted to understand the characteristics of a job or career that make it more or less attractive to Qatari students. We identified a number of job and career characteristics, and asked students to rate them on a scale from (1) "not important" to (4) "extremely important." The factors listed ranged from those that have to do with compensation such as salary and benefits, to nonpecuniary factors associated with a career, such as prestige, working hours, and job security. We first calculated averages and then ranked the responses to examine differences between males and females (Table 4.3). The responses to these questions can help elucidate how job conditions could potentially be structured to become relatively more attractive to Qataris.

Table 4.3
Importance of Factors to Choices of Job or Career

Factor	Male			Female			Total		
	Mean	Std. Err.	Rank	Mean	Std. Err.	Rank	Mean	Std. Err.	Rank
Salary	3.70	0.02	2	3.37	0.15	8	3.53	0.10	4
Bonuses	3.24	0.04	10	2.96	0.10	14	3.09	0.09	13
Health benefits	2.84	0.05	16	2.57	0.03	18	2.71	0.06	17
Retirement benefits	3.10	0.09	13	2.67	0.06	16	2.88	0.10	16
Other benefits (e.g., housing)	3.24	0.05	9	2.75	0.11	15	2.99	0.13	15
Friendly colleagues	3.06	0.07	15	3.23	0.22	10	3.14	0.13	12
Job security	3.42	0.07	6	3.44	0.11	6	3.43	0.07	6
Mixed-gender work environment	3.67	0.02	3	3.71	0.10	1	3.69	0.05	1
Women-only work environment	2.59	0.03	18	2.59	0.10	17	2.59	0.05	18
Not expected to work long hours	2.72	0.05	17	3.37	0.07	7	3.06	0.18	14
Opportunity to get more training	3.11	0.07	12	3.22	0.16	12	3.16	0.10	10
Opportunities for career advancement	3.08	0.10	14	3.22	0.14	11	3.15	0.10	11
Prestige	3.76	0.00	1	3.58	0.04	2	3.67	0.05	2
Make a contribution to society	3.29	0.08	7	3.27	0.05	9	3.28	0.04	8
Interesting work	3.48	0.07	5	3.54	0.02	4	3.51	0.04	5
Challenging work	3.28	0.05	8	3.46	0.13	5	3.37	0.08	7
Allows time to be with the family	3.22	0.04	11	3.17	0.11	13	3.20	0.06	9
Makes me feel respected and appreciated	3.56	0.02	4	3.55	0.12	3	3.55	0.06	3
Sample size	103			151			254		

NOTE: Each factor was scored by respondents as "not important" (1), "somewhat important" (2), very important" (3), "extremely important" (4), or "don't know" (0). Scores are calculated as means after dropping "don't know" responses. Sample size varies slightly across questions. Standard errors are reported.

Based on the average responses, males ranked prestige the highest, while females ranked the mixed-gender work environment the highest, followed by prestige. Among males, salary was ranked second followed by mixed-gender work environment. Females placed salary at number 8, even though at a rating of 3.37, this factor is still considered "important" to "very important." It should be noted that while the rankings give us an idea of relative importance placed on each factor by each group, none of the factors listed in Table 4.3 is unimportant—the lowest-ranked factor (women-only work environment) has a mean score of 2.59, which means that it was considered somewhere between "somewhat important" and "very important" by the average respondent.

Male respondents place greater importance than female respondents on prestige (3.76 versus 3.58, $p < 0.01$), bonuses (3.24 versus 2.96, $p < 0.05$), health benefits (2.84 versus 2.57, $p < 0.01$), retirement benefits (3.10 versus 2.67, $p < 0.01$), and other benefits (3.24 versus 2.75, $p < 0.01$), while females stated higher preference for not working long hours compared with males (3.37 versus 2.72, $p < 0.01$). Working hours was ranked at 7 for females compared with 17 for males. Males rated salary higher than females (3.70 versus 3.37), although the difference was not statistically significant at the 5-percent level ($p = 0.06$).

Other factors listed were considered equally important by both male and female respondents—differences between the averages of these items for males and females are not statistically significant. "Feeling respected on the job" was important to both males and females at ranks 4 and 3, respectively, as was how interesting the work was (ranks 5 and 4, respectively) and job security at 6 for both males and females.

These findings suggest that students look beyond factors related to monetary compensation when considering their career choices. This is important in understanding why certain jobs, such as those in the government, have traditionally been oversubscribed. The government sector is associated with greater job security, shorter working hours, and fewer working days during the year (Stasz, Eide, and Martorell, 2007; Planning Council, 2005a). The government sector also tends to structure the work environment (e.g., separate entrances, elevators, and sections) so that it is much more sensitive to local culture and traditions. The private sector may have fewer resources and flexibility (e.g., space) to do the same. Females rated the mixed-gender work environment as the most important factor, which implies that they look at this issue very closely before making a career or job choice. Paying closer attention to evolving social and cultural norms about the structure of the work environment appears to be an important strategy for increasing female participation in the workforce and another way to attract more Qataris into the private sector.

The importance given by males and females to prestige, feelings of being respected on the job, and whether the work is interesting and challenging indicate that other nonpecuniary factors related to work environment are given considerable emphasis. Furthermore, Qataris working in the government sector are automatically eligible for retirement benefits, and male Qataris are eligible for housing and social allowances. Qataris may not receive all these benefits if they chose to work in the private sector. Although policies have been adopted by some organizations in the private sector to provide these benefits to Qataris, there is little systematic data to suggest that this has become the case throughout (Planning Council, 2005a). Thus, there are important reasons why there are few Qataris employed in the private sector. Current incentives are playing a key role in terms of deciding what job or career to pursue, and where to pursue it. The private sector is forced to compete with the government sector on good salary and benefits, as well as job security, all of which are advantages that allow the government sector to employ a substantially higher share of Qataris.

While we noted the differences between males and females in terms of the importance they place on factors related to choice of job and career, we also examined these factors across groups based on plans for post-secondary study. We see some differences across the two groups, with a greater share of students who are not planning to pursue post-secondary education as rating salary ($p < 0.05$) and friendly colleagues ($p < 0.05$) "very important" or "extremely important." In terms of the remaining factors, a greater share of students not planning to pursue post-secondary study rated bonuses ($p = 0.08$) and other benefits such as housing ($p = 0.09$) as "very important" or "extremely important," although the differences were statistically significant only at the 10-percent level. The responses between the two groups on the remaining factors were not significantly different (Table 4.4).

In the next chapter, we further examine the issue of attitudes toward education, and we explore whether access to information about post-secondary options also plays a role in terms of plans after graduation.

Table 4.4
Students Rating Factors "Very Important" or "Extremely Important" in Their Choice of Job or Career (%)

Factor	Post-Secondary Education Wanted	Post-Secondary Education Not Wanted	Unsure	Total
Salary	85.4	96.5	90.4	89.7
Bonuses	70.9	83.7	69.9	74.8
Health benefits	51.0	55.8	49.0	52.3
Retirement benefits	58.5	66.1	53.9	60.3
Other benefits (e.g., housing)	56.8	66.7	73.1	62.2
Friendly colleagues	62.8	81.7	89.6	72.4
Job security	87.5	86.6	76.9	85.7
Mixed-gender work environment	95.3	96.8	95.9	95.9
Women-only work environment	50.8	51.7	53.1	51.4
Not expected to work long hours	66.3	66.4	69.5	66.8
Opportunity to get more training	73.9	74.5	82.3	75.3
Opportunities for career advancement	78.0	75.5	69.8	76.1
Prestige	93.5	92.3	92.7	93.0
Make a contribution to society	75.3	79.4	84.4	77.9
Interesting work	91.7	86.7	86.5	89.4
Challenging work	82.0	77.1	88.4	81.3
Allows time to be with the family	78.9	73.7	64.4	75.2
Makes me feel respected and appreciated	87.8	85.7	88.6	87.2
Sample size	147	71	37	255

NOTE: Sample size varies slightly across questions.

CHAPTER FIVE

Awareness and Attitudes Toward Education and Work

In this chapter, we present results from analyzing the responses of students to questions regarding their access to information and their general attitudes toward education and work. Students were asked about their familiarity with resources for receiving scholarships to attend institutions of higher learning, both in Qatar and abroad, as well as their sources of information on post-secondary education and career options. The survey assessed students' attitudes by soliciting responses to statements about education and work. The results of this analysis provide additional insight into the reasons behind the differences in the post-secondary plans and aspirations of Qatari males and females.

Familiarity with Post-Secondary Scholarship Programs

Students' awareness of available resources to further their education could be an important factor in their decision about whether or not to pursue post-secondary education. We asked students a number of questions related to the kinds of opportunities available to them in pursuing post-secondary education and training and how they obtain this information. To encourage young people to pursue higher education and training, the government of Qatar sponsors a variety of scholarship programs to study in Qatar and abroad (see Table 5.1). The most prestigious academic-based financial support available is the Emiri Scholarship, but there are also employer-based funds and scholarships for vocational study. All the scholarships are designed to encourage students to pursue academic study in prestigious institutions or in disciplines that are in high demand in Qatar, such as the science, technology (academic and vocational), and business fields.

This system has expanded recently, so we asked students whether they had heard about the scholarship opportunities available to them. Figure 5.1 illustrates the familiarity that students have with the different scholarship programs.

The findings reported in Chapter Four, Table 4.1, showed that both males and females consider getting a scholarship to be an important factor in their decision to pursue post-secondary study. A majority of the students, both males and females, have heard of the Emiri, National, and Employee Scholarship programs, as well as the Pre-College Grant and Academic Bridge programs. Fewer than half the females had heard of the Diploma Scholarship program, and about 23 percent of males and 16 percent of females had heard of all the scholarship and grant opportunities available to them. In general, females reveal slightly less familiarity with these

Table 5.1
Types of Scholarships and Enrichment Programs Available for Post-Secondary Study

Scholarship	Area of Focus or Theme	Eligibility
Emiri Scholarship	Academic excellence and promise of leadership	Student must be admitted to at least one from the list of 50 approved higher education institutions, have obtained minimum of 80 on the GSCE[a] and 530 on the TOEFL[b]
National Scholarship	Leadership in business and professional areas	Student must be admitted to at least one from the list of 250 approved higher education institutions, have obtained a minimum of 80 on the GSCE and 530 on the TOEFL
Employee Scholarship	Study in a discipline that contributes to vital and growing economic sectors, and commitment to work in specific sector; this scholarship is mainly for postgraduate study, but also for undergraduate study	Employer nomination; very good or good (in certain disciplines) undergraduate academic record; and 580 on the TOEFL
Diploma Scholarship	Study in technical or vocational field	Minimum of 65 percent on GSCE and admission to the College of the North Atlantic–Qatar
Pre-College Grant program	Additional academic preparation before pursuing post-secondary study	Minimum of 65 percent on GSCE and admission to the Academic Bridge Program

NOTE: See Supreme Education Council of Qatar (2007) for further details about eligibility for scholarship and enrichment programs.

[a] GSCE is the General Secondary Certificate Examination. It is the final exit examination administered to all government and private Arabic students in their final year of secondary study.

[b] TOEFL is the Test of English as a Foreign Language.

Figure 5.1
Student Familiarity with Scholarship Programs

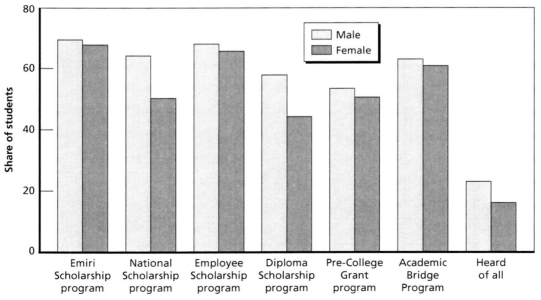

scholarship programs than males do, although the differences are only statistically significant in the case of the diploma scholarship (p < 0.01). The scholarship programs are relatively new (since 2005), and thus the level of familiarity reported by students is somewhat higher than might be expected.

Sources of Information About Jobs and Careers

Students were also asked about their sources of information concerning jobs and careers. Table 5.2 shows that more than one-third of the males cited parents and one-third cited newspapers or television as informing them about jobs and careers. This finding was similar for females: One-third cited parents and other members of their family; slightly less than one-third cited newspapers and television as their sources of information. Fewer students saw schools and teachers as sources of information on jobs and careers. This is an area that could be a target for improvement; schools and teachers could be an effective means of communicating job and career options for students, particularly in terms of establishing a clearer link between academic success and prospective career choices.

The establishment of the Higher Education Institute (HEI) is a step in that direction. The HEI provides counseling and career advice for secondary school students, manages the scholarship programs, and sets standards that qualify the post-secondary institutions where the scholarships can be applied (Brewer et al., 2007; Supreme Education Council, 2008a). The HEI might endeavor to forge better links with schools to assist in meeting its objectives of addressing labor market needs, preparing talented students for leadership roles, and increasing the number of students pursuing careers in high-demand fields (Supreme Education Council, 2008a).

Perceptions About the Value of Education and Work

We included several statements concerning job and career in the questionnaire and asked students to "strongly disagree," "disagree," "strongly agree," or "agree" with these statements.

Table 5.2
Sources of Information on Jobs and Careers (%)

Source of Information	Male	Female	Total
School	15.1	20.2	17.7
Teachers	11.6	6.4	9.0
Parents	36.7	33.0	34.8
Other members of my family	23.1	33.4	28.4
Friends	25.8	20.6	23.1
Newspapers or television	33.7	29.0	31.3
Other	1.7	1.7	1.7
I do not have an answer	4.7	4.9	4.8
Sample size	103	150	253

NOTE: Sample size varies slightly across questions.

These statements were intended to ascertain attitudes toward education and work and to provide further insight into how those attitudes might influence post-secondary plans.

Table 5.3 illustrates the percentage of students who responded "strongly agree" or "agree" to the statements posed. Note that while there are similarities between males and females, there are also some important differences. About 95 percent of both males and females affirmed the importance of getting a good education. A slightly larger share of males reported that getting good grades at school would help an individual get a better job (97 versus 90 percent), while a larger share of females than males worried about getting a job they like (85 percent versus 73 percent). In both cases the differences were only significant at close to the 10-percent level (respectively, $p = 0.07$ and $p = 0.09$). Even more important in terms of differences between males' and females' views about school and work is that, while more than 90 percent of females agree or strongly agree that more job opportunities should be available to women and that women should be allowed to work outside the home, only 63 percent and 53 percent of males, respectively, felt the same way on these issues ($p < 0.01$). A greater share of males compared with females (87 versus 77 percent) agreed or strongly agreed with the statement that studying a technical field is associated with higher salaries ($p < 0.01$). Up until recently, technical fields have not been open to women in Qatar, and thus it is important to understand the underlying context in the response to this question.

Although 54 percent of males agreed or strongly agreed that you have to go outside of Qatar to get a good education compared with only 43 percent of females, this difference was not statistically significant ($p = 0.35$). This was also the case with the statement that "who you know is more important than what you know"; similar shares of males and females (54 percent of males and 57 percent of females, $p = 0.77$) agreed or strongly agreed.

Table 5.3
Views Toward School and Work, by Gender, 2006 Cohort

Statement	Percentage Agreeing or Strongly Agreeing with Statement		
	Male	Female	Total
It is important to get a good education	94.7	94.7	94.7
Getting good grades at school helps you get a better job	96.6	89.8	93.1
You worry about getting a job that you will like	72.7	85.3	79.3
You have to go abroad to get the best education	54.1	43.1	48.3
People think better of you if you have a university degree	81.3	75.8	78.4
A job is not as important as the family	58.8	61.6	60.2
There should be more jobs open to women	62.7	93.8	78.7
The best jobs in Qatar are in the government (civil service)	77.7	70.7	74.1
People who study a technical field (e.g., engineering) can get a high-paying job	87.1	76.6	81.6
Work is harder in private companies than in government jobs	62.3	54.6	58.3
To get a good job, who you know is more important than what you know	54.0	56.7	55.4
Women should be able to work outside the home	52.9	94.4	74.5
Sample Size	103	151	254

NOTE: Sample size varies slightly across questions.

The results of this analysis suggest that both males and females place importance on getting a quality education and performing well in school, and associate these two endeavors with positive life outcomes. In the case of males, as we found in our earlier analysis, getting a good job may have little to do with their decision to pursue post-secondary study, or they may prefer to gain education and training through their jobs.

We noted earlier that male survey respondents tended to view their job prospects more favorably than did the female survey respondents. We know that males and females share similar views on the value of education, and they both place importance on parental guidance and working conditions in making decisions about a post-secondary career. The difference between males and females appears to be primarily in how they view their options, which may explain why there are significant differences in the choices they ultimately end up making.

These differences are also evident in the responses of males relative to females in their perceptions of the job opportunities available to them and their confidence that they will get the job they want. Males and females responded very differently on these dimensions. Table 5.4 illustrates these differences: 76 percent of males are very certain that they will get the job they want, compared with 59 percent of females (p < 0.01).

The difference between males' and females' perceptions about job prospects is even more apparent in a comparison of post-secondary education plans. Of the males who were very certain they would be able to get the job they want, only 43 percent planned on going on to post-secondary study (Table 5.5). In stark contrast, of the females who were very certain they would get the job they wanted, up to 80 percent were planning to continue on to post-secondary study.

These results suggest that males do not deem obtaining a post-secondary degree a condition to getting the job that they want, either because many careers they aspire to do not require a post-secondary degree or because they see themselves as being competitive despite lacking a post-secondary qualification. Males simply do not face the same incentives to pursue post-secondary education as females do. This may be attributed to males' job guarantee of joining the military or police, an attractive employment option that does not require a post-secondary degree.

Table 5.4
Students' Self-Confidence in Getting the Job They Want (%)

Statement	Male	Female	Total
Very certain	75.7	58.5	66.7
Somewhat certain	18.5	32.1	25.6
Not certain	0.0	2.3	1.2
Don't know	2.9	5.3	4.1
Do not plan to enter workforce	0.5	0.0	0.3
Don't have answer	2.4	1.9	2.1
Sample size	102	152	254

Table 5.5
Gender Differences in Job-Attainment Confidence, by Post-Secondary Plan (%)

Post-Secondary Plan	Job Attainment Confidence			
	Very Certain	Somewhat Certain	Not Certain	Total
Males				
Post-secondary education wanted	42.9	40.4	0.0	42.4
Post-secondary education not wanted	45.6	50.3	0.0	46.6
Unsure	11.5	9.3	0.0	11.1
Sample size	77	19	0	96
Females				
Post-secondary education wanted	79.7	54.2	45.6	70.0
Post-secondary education not wanted	9.6	21.7	45.6	14.6
Unsure	10.8	24.1	8.7	15.3
Sample size	85	52	5	142

CHAPTER SIX

Conclusions

This report presents data from a sample of Qatari secondary school seniors on their post-secondary goals and aspirations, their attitudes about school and work, and their access to information on post-secondary options. It also highlights the main findings of Qatari student survey responses, to provide policymakers and researchers with an understanding of the decisions they make, how this varies across males and females, and the main drivers behind those decisions. The results of this analysis could help Qatar's decisionmakers structure incentives that lead to desirable post-secondary and labor market outcomes.

Analysis of the survey results may support earlier findings that career opportunities for females are improving (Bahry and Marr, 2005). Females are beginning to favor occupations in the professional fields that were traditionally reserved for males. In general, both males and females value the same factors when considering jobs, and they appear to rely on the same resources for information about career options. Both view working conditions; social influences, such as the advice of parents; and prestige associated with the job as important determinants when deciding on a career.

Nonetheless, there are important differences between males and females in terms of their post-secondary plans: While males and females value education equally, males are significantly less likely to plan to go on to post-secondary study than females are. We explored these differences more closely because the decision on the part of males to forgo post-secondary education in favor of entering the workforce has important implications for the supply of Qatari human capital to sectors identified by the nation's leaders as important targets for growth.

We analyzed a number of factors that might explain this difference. On the face of it, males and females place importance on the same types of job characteristics, so this would not explain why the difference exists. Similar proportions of male and female respondents reported familiarity with scholarships to fund higher education, and both males and females appear to rely less on their schools and teachers for advice about career options and more on their parents, relatives, and the media. The main difference lies in how males and females perceive their job prospects. Males appear much more confident they will get the job they want, regardless of whether they pursue post-secondary education or not. Females, on the other hand, appear relatively less confident that their current abilities will get them the jobs they want without pursuing higher education. Incentives do not appear to encourage males to pursue further education and training, at least prior to entering the workforce. Males may expect to receive training after they have acquired a job—either through an employer-sponsored plan or directly from the employer.

Education reform initiatives meant to address these issues should be coupled with labor market reforms to support them. As long as the association between education and training and labor market outcomes remains tenuous, it is unlikely that the K–12 and higher education reforms in which the nation has invested will have their intended impact. This study provides evidence that post-secondary decisions may be driven by factors that make such study appear less appealing and benefit-conferring to males than choosing an occupation that will provide them with training opportunities, prestige, appropriate working conditions, and job security. Consequently, to attract more males, the incentives to continue into post-secondary education and training should be restructured to make that path more appealing relative to directly entering the job market.

Concomitantly, barriers to female labor force participation need to be further examined. As this study shows, the significantly larger percentage of women than men who plan to go on to post-secondary study suggests that increasing the share of Qataris in the government enterprise and private sectors will have a lot to do with addressing existing barriers to female labor-force participation, whether they are personal, cultural, or employer-based. Policymakers could mount campaigns to increase awareness of the opportunities available to women and the societal benefits of female workforce participation. Employers and higher education institutions could also support the appointment and training of guidance counseling services in the secondary schools to increase awareness of career and professional opportunities among Qatari students.

As Qatar's economy continues to grow and more professional and career opportunities are created for its citizens, it will be instructive to conduct periodic studies to help identify appropriate strategies to meet the country's growing demand for a skilled national labor force. The results of the survey of secondary school seniors presented in this report highlight the importance of understanding the underlying factors affecting the decisions of soon-to-be graduates of the K–12 secondary school system. Labor force participation and unemployment data are systematically collected in Qatar through existing labor force surveys, although the data do not provide information on attitudes and perceptions affecting employment decisions of young Qataris. Anecdotal evidence gathered through conversations with employers and post-secondary education officials provides an important perspective on post-secondary decision-making behavior and the reasons behind it, but it limits the inferences needed to put new policies into effect. Effective policymaking to motivate certain behaviors can only come about through the use of detailed systematic data on people's perceptions, the factors shaping those perceptions, and the incentive structures they face when making life choices such as those related to education and work. The survey of secondary school seniors and the analytical results presented in this paper should be the first in a regular systematic assessment of attitudes and perceptions of the future Qatari workforce.

High School Student Questionnaire

On the following pages, we reproduce the English version of the questionnaire. An Arabic translation was administered to Qatari secondary school seniors.

This questionnaire asks questions about you, your family, your goals for the future, and other topics to help us understand how high school seniors think about their future.

This information will be used in research project conducted by RAND, a private, non-profit research institute, for the Supreme Education Council. The aim of the project is to help the Council develop priorities for the education and training opportunities that are available in Qatar. If you have any questions about the study, please ask the proctor.

Answering this questionnaire is voluntary. We hope that you will take the survey and answer the questions. If you do not wish to answer a question or do not know the answer, mark the box for "I do not have an answer."

We are not asking for your name, so no one will know the answers you personally give.

THIS QUESTIONNAIRE IS FOR STUDENTS WHO ARE 18 YEARS OLD OR OLDER. IF

YOU WERE NOT AT LEAST 18 YEARS OLD ON YOUR LAST BIRTHDAY, PLEASE TELL

THE PROCTOR. YOU DO NOT NEED TO COMPLETE THIS QUESTIONNAIRE.

SECTION I: YOUR BACKGROUND

First, a few questions about you and what you are studying in school.

1. What is your date of birth?   _____/_____/_____   /1/ ⬚
                                     (month) (day) (year)

2. Are you male or female? (circle one number below)   /2/ ⬚
     1. Male
     2. Female

3. What is your country of nationality? (circle one number below)   /3/ ⬚
     1. Qatari

     2. Non Qatari

     3. Please Specify _____

4. What is your main course of study in school?   /4/ ⬚
        (circle one number below)

     1.   Literature and humanities

     2.   Science and mathematics

     3.   Other _____ (please describe)

     4.   I do not have an answer

5. What grade are you in this year? (circle one number below)   /5/ ⬚
     1.   Grade 11
     2.   Grade 12
     3.   I do not have an answer

6. Is this your first year in this grade? (circle one number below)   /6/ ⬚
     1.   Yes, this is my first time in this grade

     2.   No, I am repeating this grade

     3.   I do not have an answer

7. What is your FATHER's highest level of education?   /7/ ⬚
        (circle one number below)

     1.   Never attended school

     2.   Primary (grades 1 — 6)

     3.   Preparatory (grades 7-9)

     4.   Secondary (grades 10-12)

     5.   Pre-university diploma

     6.   Bachelor's degree

     7.   Master's degree

     8.   Doctorate or other higher degree

     9.   I do not have an answer

8. What is your MOTHER's highest level of education?   /8/□
(circle one number below)

1.   Never attended school

2.   Primary (grades 1 — 6)

3.   Preparatory (grades 7-9)

4.   Secondary (grades 10-12)

5.   Pre-university diploma

6.   Bachelor's degree

7.   Master's degree

8.   Doctorate or other higher degree

9.   I do not have an answer

SECTION II: YOUR FUTURE GOALS

Now we have some questions about your plans for the future. There are no right or wrong answers to these questions. We just want to learn about your plans and views.

9. After graduating from high school do you plan to: /9/ ☐
   (circle one number below)

1.   Go to university

2.   Go to technical college

3.   Go to work right after high school

4.   Remain at home—not attend university/school or look for work

5.   Not sure what I will do

6.   None of the above, I plan to _____
      (please describe)

7.   I do not have an answer

How important are each of the following factors in your choice of what you will do after you graduate from high school?

(circle one number in each row)

Category	Not Important	Somewhat Important	Very Important	Extremely Important	I do not have an answer	
a. My own personal interests	1	2	3	4	0	/10.1/ ☐
b. Advice from my father or mother	1	2	3	4	0	/10.2/ ☐
c. Advice from other family members	1	2	3	4	0	/10.3/ ☐
d. Advice from my friends	1	2	3	4	0	/10.4/ ☐
e. My religious beliefs	1	2	3	4	0	/10.5/ ☐
f. What society expects of me	1	2	3	4	0	/10.6/ ☐
g. My enjoyment of learning and school	1	2	3	4	0	/10.7/ ☐
h. The kinds of jobs that are open to me	1	2	3	4	0	/10.8/ ☐
i. Whether I get a scholarship	1	2	3	4	0	/10.9/ ☐

10.   **Have you heard about the following scholarship programs that are available in Qatar?**

(circle one answer for each)

The Emiri Scholarship program	YES	NO	/11.1/ ☐
The National Scholarship program	YES	NO	/11.2/ ☐
The Employee Scholarship program	YES	NO	/11.3/ ☐
The Diploma Scholarship program	YES	NO	/11.4/ ☐
The Pre-college Grant program	YES	NO	/11.5/ ☐
The Academic Bridge program	YES	NO	/11.6/ ☐
I do not have an answer	☐		/11.7/ ☐

11.   **What kind of job would you MOST like to have?**   /12/☐

(Please write your answer here OR circle one number below)

_____

1.   Not sure what job I want

2.   I do not plan to get a job

3.   I do not have an answer

12.   **What do you think you need to do to prepare for the kind of job or career you would MOST like to have?** (circle one number below)
/13/ ☐

1.   Get a university degree in Qatar (e.g., bachelors, masters or doctoral degree)

2.   Go abroad for university

3.   Get another type of qualification (e.g., technical certificate or diploma)

4.   Get some work experience related to the job I want.

5.   I won't need further preparation for the job I want

6.   Not sure what preparation I will need

7.   Other _____ (please describe)

8.   Do not plan to enter the workforce

9.   I do not have an answer

13.   **Once you begin looking for a job, in what kind of organization**   /14/ ☐
      would you <u>MOST</u> like to work? (circle one number below)

    1.   For the government (e.g. Ministry of Education)

    2.   For a company or organization the government owns or
       partially owns (e.g., Qatar Petroleum)

    3.   For a privately-owned charitable or religious organization

    4.   For a privately-owned company owned by my family

    5.   For a privately-owned company **not** owned by my family

    6.   Other _____ (please describe)

    7.   Not sure where I want to work

    8.   Do not plan to enter the workforce

    9.   I do not have an answer

14.   **Where do you get information about how to prepare for jobs or
careers?**

       I get this information from: (circle all that apply)
    1.   the school I attend   /15.1/☐
    2.   my teachers   /15.2/☐
    3.   my parents   /15.3/☐
    4.   other members of my family   /15.4/☐
    5.   my friends   /15.5/☐
    6.   newspapers or television   /15.6/☐
    7.   other sources _____ (please describe) /15.7/☐
    8.   I do not have an answer   /15.8/☐

15.   In thinking about a future job, how important to you is each of
       the following characteristics in your choice of a job?

(circle one number in each row)

Category	Not Important	Somewhat Important	Very Important	Extremely Important	I do not have an answer		
Salary	1	2	3	4	0	/1/	☐
Bonuses	1	2	3	4	0	/2/	☐
Health benefits	1	2	3	4	0	/3/	☐
Retirement benefits	1	2	3	4	0	/4/	☐
Other benefits (e.g. housing)	1	2	3	4	0	/5/	☐
Friendly colleagues	1	2	3	4	0	/6/	☐
Job security	1	2	3	4	0	/7/	☐
Mixed-gender work environment	1	2	3	4	0	/8/	☐
Women-only work environment	1	2	3	4	0	/9/	☐
Are not expected to work long hours	1	2	3	4	0	/10/	☐
Opportunity to get more training	1	2	3	4	0	/11/	☐
Opportunities for career advancement	1	2	3	4	0	/12/	☐
Prestige	1	2	3	4	0	/13/	☐
Make a contribution to society	1	2	3	4	0	/14/	☐
Interesting work	1	2	3	4	0	/15/	☐
Challenging work	1	2	3	4	0	/16/	☐
Allows time to be with the family	1	2	3	4	0	/17/	☐
Makes me feel respected and appreciated	1	2	3	4	0	/18/	☐

16.   How certain do you feel about your ability to achieve the kind of
      job or career that you want?
                              (circle one number below)   /17/☐
      1.   very certain
      2.   somewhat certain
      3.   not certain
      4.   don't know
      5.   do not plan to enter the workforce
      6.   I do not have an answer

17.   Which of the following factors do you think might help or support
      you, or which might prevent you, from achieving the kind of job
      or career that you want?

                    (circle one number in each row)

Category	Will prevent me	Will neither help nor prevent	Will help me	I do not have an answer		
My personal interests	1	2	3	0	/1/	☐
My parents	1	2	3	0	/2/	☐
Other members of my family	1	2	3	0	/3/	☐
My friends	1	2	3	0	/4/	☐
My school or teachers	1	2	3	0	/5/	☐
My grades in school	1	2	3	0	/6/	☐
My exam scores	1	2	3	0	/7/	☐
My willingness to work hard	1	2	3	0	/8/	☐
Family obligations	1	2	3	0	/9/	☐
Societal views about women in the workforce	1	2	3	0	/10/	☐
Personal contacts	1	2	3	0	/11/	☐
What I studied in school (e.g., literature or science stream)	1	2	3	0	/12/	☐
My ability to speak English	1	2	3	0	/13/	☐
My ability to get along with other people	1	2	3	0	/14/	☐

18.   **Finally, do you agree or disagree with the following statements about school and work.**

(circle one number in each row)

Category	Strongly disagree	Disagree	Agree	Strongly agree	I do not have an answer		
It is important to get a good education	1	2	3	4	0	/1/	☐
Getting good grades at school helps you get a better job	1	2	3	4	0	/2/	☐
I worry about getting a job that I will like	1	2	3	4	0	/3/	☐
You have to go abroad to get the best education	1	2	3	4	0	/4/	☐
People think better of you if you have a university degree	1	2	3	4	0	/5/	☐
A job is not as important as the family	1	2	3	4	0	/6/	☐
There should be more jobs open to women	1	2	3	4	0	/7/	☐
The best jobs in Qatar are in the government (civil service)	1	2	3	4	0	/8/	☐
People who study a technical field (e.g., engineering) can get a higher paying job.	1	2	3	4	0	/9/	☐
Work is harder in private companies than in government jobs	1	2	3	4	0	/10/	☐
To get a good job, who you know is more important than what you know	1	2	3	4	0	/11/	☐
Women should be able to work outside the home	1	2	3	4	0	/12/	☐

THANK YOU VERY MUCH FOR TAKING THE TIME TO COMPLETE THIS QUESTIONNAIRE.

Weighting the Sample

Survey responses were weighted to reflect the distribution of 18-year-olds across the different types of schools in Qatar. We used data from the MoE to determine the number of 18-year-olds during the period of the survey administration across all school types in Qatar.

We constructed sample weights using the following formula:

$$w_s = \frac{1}{N} \frac{a_S^{POP}}{a_S^{SAMP}}$$

Each student observation is weighted by w_s, with s representing the school that the student is enrolled in. N is the sample size, a_S^{POP} is the share of the students enrolled in school s out of the total population of students (who were 18 years old or older) during the period of the survey administration), and a_S^{SAMP} is the share of students in school s out of the total sample of students. A student from a school that was oversampled will be weighted downward because that student represents a larger share of the sample, and vice versa for students who were undersampled relative to the population. Weights were calculated by gender and school type. The resulting weights were used in the data analysis (see Table B.1).

Table B.1
Sample Weights, by Gender and Type of School

Type of School	Total Number of Qataris Meeting Criteria		Number in Sample		Calculated Sample Weight	
	Male	Female	Male	Female	Male	Female
Private Arabic	21	—	6	—	0.00246132	—
Ministry of Education	580	674	74	110	0.00551184	0.00430891
Independent, Generation I	4	7	4	7	0.00070323	0.00070323
Independent, Generation II	84	52	23	36	0.00256834	0.00101578
Total	689	733	107	153		

References

Bahry, Louay, and Phebe Marr (2005). "Qatari Women: A New Generation of Leaders?" *Middle East Policy,* Vol. 12, No. 2.

Brewer, Dominic J., Catherine H. Augustine, Gail L. Zellman, Gery Ryan, Charles A. Goldman, Cathleen Stasz, and Louay Constant (2007). *Education for a New Era: Design and Implementation of K–12 Education Reform in Qatar.* Santa Monica, Calif.: RAND Corporation, MG-548-QATAR. As of March 1, 2008: http://www.rand.org/pubs/monographs/MG548/

DeRidder, Larry (1990). *The Impact of Parents and Parenting on Career Development.* Knoxville, Tenn.: Comprehensive Career Development Project.

General Secretariat for Development Planning, State of Qatar (2007). *Qatar Statistics.* As of March 13, 2008: http://www.planning.gov.qa/statistics.html

Gouvias, Dionyssios, and C. Vitsilakis-Soroniatis (2005). "Student Employment and Parental Influences on Educational and Occupational Aspirations of Greek Adolescents." *Journal of Education and Work,* Vol. 18, No. 4, pp. 421–449.

Government of Qatar, Education, Embassy of the State of Qatar in Washington, D.C. As of April 1, 2008: http://www.qatarembassy.net/education.asp

Jolo, Hend (2004). *Human Capital Formation in the State of Qatar with Special Reference to Oil and Gas Based Industries.* Doctoral dissertation, Exeter, UK: University of Exeter.

Martorell, Francisco, and Vazha Nadareishvili, with Hanine Salem (2008). *A Survey of Recent Qatar High School Graduates: Methods and Results.* Santa Monica, Calif.: RAND Corporation, TR-578-QATAR. As of May 2008: www.rand.org/pubs/technical_reports/TR578/

The Minnesota High School Follow-Up Survey (2000). *A Digest of Information Based on the Education Experiences of the Minnesota High School Classes of 1997–1999, Trend Report.* St. Paul, Minn.: Minnesota State Department of Children, Families, and Learning.

——— (2001). *Post-Secondary Education Choices of the Minnesota High School Class of 1999.* St. Paul, Minn.: Minnesota Higher Education Services Office.

Mortimer, Jeylan T., Katherine Dennehy, and Chaimun Lee (1992). *Influences on Adolescents' Vocational Development.* Berkeley, Calif.: National Center for Research in Vocational Education, University of California, MDS-268.

Mullis, Iva V.S., Michael O. Martin, Eugenio J. Gonzalez, and Steven J. Chrostowski (2004). *Findings from IEA's Trends in International Mathematics and Science Study at the Fourth and Eighth Grades.* Chestnut Hill, Mass.: TIMSS & PIRLS International Study Center, Boston College. As of September 12, 2007: http://isc.bc.edu/timss2003i/mathD.html

Need, Ariana, and Uulkje de Jong (2001). "Educational Differentials in the Netherlands." *Rationality and Society,* Vol. 13, No. 1, pp. 71–98.

Planning Council, State of Qatar (2005a). *A Labour Market Strategy for the State of Qatar: Main Report,* Vol. 1.

————— (2005b). *Annual Abstract: 2005.* Doha, Qatar: State of Qatar Planning Council. As of August 22, 2006:
http://www.planning.gov.qa/AnnAbs/annabst_2005/annabst/2005/First-Section/LabourFource/Labour_Index.htm

Qatar Foundation for Education, Science, and Community Development (2008). "Education." As of January 20, 2008:
http://www.qf.org.qa/output/page307.asp

Qatar Ministry of Education (2005). *Ministry of Education Annual Statistics Report 2004/2005,* Doha, Qatar: Ministry of Education.

Qatar University (2007). *The Reform Project.* As of September 11, 2007:
http://www.qu.edu.qa/html/reformproject.html

Stasz, Cathleen, Eric Eide, and Francisco Martorell (2007). *Post-Secondary Education in Qatar: Employer Demand, Student Choice, and Options for Policy,* Santa Monica, Calif.: RAND Corporation, MG-644-QATAR. As of March 13, 2008:
http://www.rand.org/pubs/monographs/MG644/

Supreme Education Council of Qatar (2007). *Scholarship Programs.* As of September 11, 2007:
http://www.english.education.gov.qa/section/sec/hei/sco

————— (2008a). *Higher Education Institute.* As of January 20, 2008:
http://www.english.education.gov.qa/section/sec/hei

————— (2008b). *Independent Schools.* As of May 11, 2008:
http://www.english.education.gov.qa/schools/EISsearch.htm